Baked Beans

Written by Jane Wood

Contents

Where do baked beans come from?	2
How are baked beans made?	6
Eating baked beans	10
How to grow haricot beans	12
Glossary	15
Index	16

D0186169

Where do baked beans come from?

Baked beans are made from **haricot** beans.

This field is full of haricot bean plants.

The beans grow in **pods** on the plants.

Beans need rain and sunshine to grow.

3

The beans are picked
when they are
dry and ripe.

The beans are taken
to the **factory**.
At the factory,
they will be made
into baked beans.

How are baked beans made?

First the beans are sorted

by size and colour.

Then they are washed.

Next the beans are soaked in hot water. This makes them soft.

Then tomato sauce is made.

Then the beans
are put into cans
and covered
in tomato sauce.

Next the beans are **sealed** in the cans.

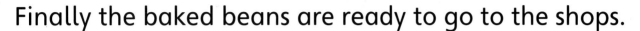

The cans are cooked and then cooled.

Finally the baked beans are ready to go to the shops.

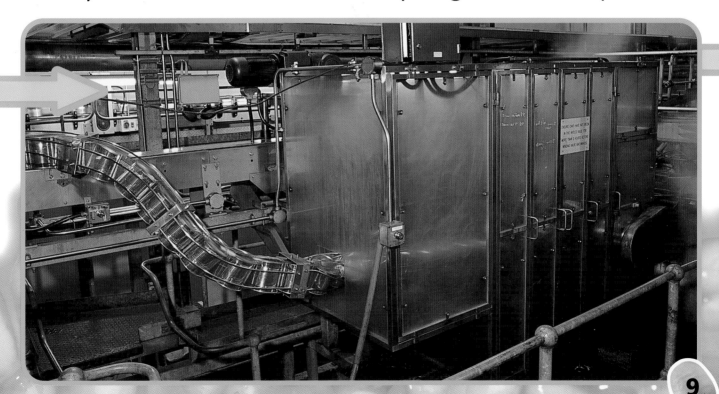

Eating baked beans

Baked beans are good for you.

They help you run fast

and work hard.

Meals with baked beans

Baked beans are very easy to cook.

You just heat them up.

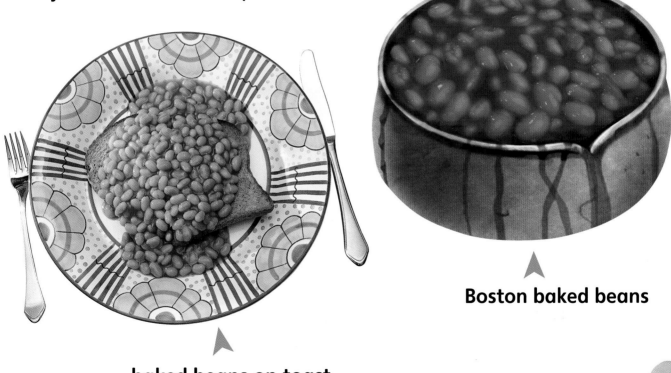

baked beans on toast

Boston baked beans

How to grow haricot beans

1 In spring, plant the beans 5 centimetres deep.

2 Water them at least once a day.

3

Give the plants

some sticks to lean on.

They will soon get to the top.

13

4

The beans will be ready to eat in the summer.

Glossary

Boston baked beans - an American recipe

for baked beans

factory - a building where things are made

haricot - the kind of bean used to make

baked beans

pods - a part of a plant where beans grow

sealed - closed so that air cannot get in

Index

canning beans 8-9

cooking beans 11

eating beans 10

factory 5

growing beans 2-3, 12-14

picking beans 4

sorting beans 6

tomato sauce 7, 8

washing beans 6